D1305020

TOMBS & TREASURES

CATHERINE CHARLEY

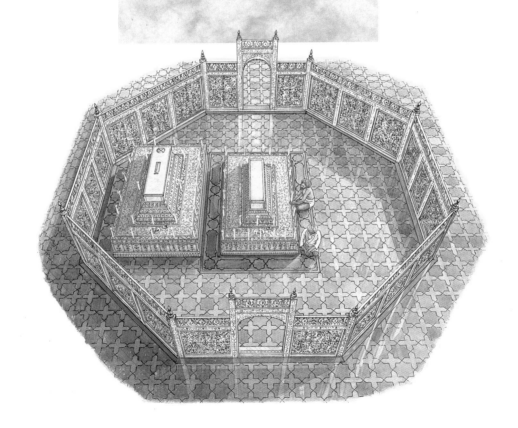

Viking

j930.1
CHA
C.1

Acknowledgments

**The publishers would like to thank Jonathan Adams, who illustrated the
see-through pages; James Field, who illustrated the cover; and the organizations and
individuals that have given their permission to reproduce the following pictures:**

Accademia Italiana/© Soprintendente, Pompeii: 21 top.
Ancient Art and Architecture Collection: 12, 29 top center, 29 top left, 29 top right, 38, 39 bottom.
Ashmolean Museum, Oxford: 5, 13 top.
Bridgeman Art Library: 36 bottom, /British Museum: 8 top right, 8 top left, 15, 32.
British Museum: 33 top right.
D. Donne Bryant Stock Photography/D. Donne Bryant: 30 top,
/Museo del Banco Central del Ecuador, Quito 39 top.
Christies Images: 36 top, 37 top.
Cultural Relics Bureau/Metropolitan Museum of Art, New York: 19.
C.M. Dixon/British Museum: 26 bottom, 35 bottom, /Hermitage Museum, St. Petersburg 13 center.
Explorer: 16, /J.P. Courau 23 bottom center, 30 bottom right, /René Mattes 42 top right.
Werner Forman Archive/The Greenland Museum: 42 top left.
Robert Harding Picture Library: 7 top left, 18 top, 18 bottom, 30 bottom left, /Heinze Plenge 23 bottom right,
/Adam Woolfitt 40 top right. **Hirmer Verlag:** 10.
Michael Holford Photographs/British Museum: 14, 33 top center. **National Museum of Ireland:** 27.
Master and Fellows of Magdalene College: 40 top left. **Mary Rose Trust:** 40 bottom.
Marion & Tony Morrison/South American Pictures: 23 bottom left.
National Geographic Society Image Collection/O.L. Mazzatenta: 39 top.
Römisch-Germanisches Zentralmuseum: 43 top, 43 bottom.
Scala: 7 top right, 20, 45, /Museo Nazionale, Naples 21 bottom.
V&A Picture Library: 44. **Vladimir Vitanov Agency:** 26 top.
Weidenfeld and Nicolson Archive/R. Skelton: 35 top.

Illustrators
Jonathan Adams: 9, 17, 24–25, 41.
Richard Berridge (Specs Art): 8, 12, 13, 14, 16 top, 26–27, 36–37.
James Field: cover.
Terry Gabbey (Associated Freelance Artists): 20, 21, 42, 43.
André Hrydziuszko: 15, 34–35, 44–45.
Joe Lawrence: 4, 5, 16 bottom, 18, 29 bottom right, plus all
map and heading icons and endpapers.
Kevin Madison: 10, 11, 32–33.
Angus McBride (Linden Artists): 6, 7, 19, 22, 23, 28,
29 bottom right, 31, 38, 46–47.

Viking
Published by the Penguin Group
Penguin USA, 375 Hudson Street, New York, New York 10014, U.S.A.
Penguin Books Ltd, 27 Wrights Lane, London W8 5TZ, England
Penguin Books Australia Ltd, Ringwood, Victoria, Australia
Penguin Books Canada Ltd, 10 Alcorn Avenue, Toronto, Ontario, Canada M4V 3B2
Penguin Books (N.Z.) Ltd, 182–190 Wairau Road, Auckland 10, New Zealand

Penguin Books Ltd, Registered Offices: Harmondsworth, Middlesex, England

First published in Great Britain by Hamlyn Children's Books,
an imprint of Reed Children's Books Limited, 1994
First published in the United States of America by Viking,
a division of Penguin USA, 1995

1 3 5 7 9 10 8 6 4 2

Copyright © Reed International Books Limited, 1994

All rights reserved

ISBN 0–670–85899–4

Printed in Belgium

Without limiting the rights under copyright reserved above, no part of this
publication may be reproduced, stored in or introduced into a retrieval system,
or transmitted, in any form or by any means (electronic, mechanical,
photocopying, recording or otherwise), without the prior written permission
of both the copyright owner and the above publisher of this book.

CONTENTS

Tombs and Treasures 4
Tutankhamen 6
The Cemetery at Ur 8
The Etruscans 10
Scythian Tombs 12
The First Mausoleum 14
Philip of Macedonia 16
The Jade Prince 18
Pompeii 20
The Lords of Sipán 22
Old and New Lords 24
Invasion Treasures 26
The Terracotta Army 28
The Tomb of Pacal 30
Sutton Hoo 32
Tamerlane 34
Spanish Treasure 36
El Dorado 38
The *Mary Rose* 40
Preserved Bodies 42
The Taj Mahal 44
Key Dates and Glossary 46
Index 48

TOMBS AND TREASURES

Throughout history, humans have treated their dead with great respect and in special ways. Even the primitive Neanderthal people of the Stone Age are known to have buried their dead in shallow graves, over 35,000 years ago.

BURIAL CUSTOMS
Over the centuries, different peoples have developed their own burial customs. The ceremony following a death often reflected a people's way of life. Seafarers, such as the Vikings, sometimes placed their dead leaders in boats that were then pushed out to sea, burned, or buried. They believed that the dead person would go on a great journey to a new life after death. Some other cultures did not bury their dead at all. The Tibetans gave their relations a "sky" burial, chopping up the bodies during a ceremony and leaving them for the vultures. This was because all fertile land in the high Himalayan mountains was needed for growing food.

TOMBS
Burial places, or tombs, have varied from natural caves to splendid monuments. The most elaborate tombs were usually for the richest and highest ranking people. Frequently the dead were buried with their most important possessions. For example, a warrior king would have his armor and weapons, while a rich prince or princess was given objects of gold, silver, and other precious goods. Even the graves of poor people have been found with hunting equipment or cooking utensils.

In many cultures it was believed that these goods would be needed in a new life after death. In some tombs, the bodies of servants have been found, ready to serve their master or mistress in the new life.

The dead are often buried in a container called a coffin or sarcophagus. Oak coffins made from a hollowed tree trunk 3,000 years ago have been found in Denmark, and ancient 4,000-year-old clay coffins have been discovered in Iraq.

Spanish treasure

The tomb of Pacal

El Dorado

The Lords of Sipán

TREASURES
Not all buried treasures are found in tombs. Valuable objects have been discovered in many places, probably buried before a war or an invasion or during a revolution. Others may simply have been lost, swept away, or buried by natural disasters.

HISTORICAL EVIDENCE

For historians and archaeologists, many types of objects, not just gold and precious items, are treasures. For them, looking at the tombs and treasures of past societies is like opening a window on their daily life and culture. Unfortunately, archaeologists have to contend with some treasure hunters, who, having little interest in the surrounding evidence, destroy our links with the past. In this book you will find out about some of the world's most interesting tombs and treasures, how they came to be there, and how they were found.

Many valuable objects have been found that were probably buried during a war or an invasion and never recovered by the owners. Other treasures, such as the Alfred Jewel (above), found in a marsh in England, might have just been lost. It has been suggested that King Alfred of England once owned the jewel.

The *Mary Rose*

Ötzi

Scythian tombs

The tomb of Tutankhamen

The tomb of Tamerlane

The Taj Mahal

The Jade Prince

The Terracotta Army

Sutton Hoo

Invasion treasures

Etruscan tombs

Pompeii

The tomb of Philip of Macedonia

The Mausoleum at Halicarnassus

The royal cemetery at Ur

This map shows the location of the main tombs and treasures described in this book.

5

TUTANKHAMEN

On November 4, 1922, the most famous steps in archaeology were discovered. They led toward a 3,000- year-old door, and the tomb of the Egyptian pharaoh Tutankhamen.

THE DISCOVERY

The 16 steps had lain hidden under piles of rubble for centuries. As archaeologist Howard Carter and his sponsor, Lord Carnarvon, removed more debris from the door, they were thrilled to uncover Tutankhamen's name. But they also found that the door had been opened and resealed twice, and feared that the tomb had been looted of its treasures long ago.

> At first I could see nothing, the hot air escaping from the chamber causing the candle to flicker, but presently, as my eyes grew accustomed to the light, details of the room within emerged slowly from the mist, strange animals, statues, and gold—everywhere there was a glint of gold.
>
> — *Howard Carter* —

Beyond, they found a passage leading to a second door. Carter peered through a gap at the top of it. "Can you see anything?" asked Lord Carnarvon impatiently from behind him. "Yes," replied Carter in a whisper. "Wonderful things. Strange animals, statues, and gold." Shining treasures glittered in the candlelight. The five-year search for Tutankhamen's tomb was over.

antechamber, containing couches, chariot, and throne

annex, containing food, oils, and wines

corridor

The four chambers of Tutankhamen's tomb. The first pharaohs were placed in enormous pyramids when they died, but these tombs were easily identified and robbed. By Tutankhamen's time, the pharaohs were buried in underground tombs in an isolated valley. Although thieves had broken into his tomb, they probably stole only a few small, but still very valuable, items.

burial chamber, with mummy in shrines and coffins

treasury, containing funeral gifts and religious objects

Tutankhamen's gold throne. On its back is a picture of Tutankhamen and his wife made out of semi-precious stones and colored glass.

THE DEATH OF THE KING

Tutankhamen had died in 1323 B.C. at the age of eighteen. Like most pharaohs, he was mummified to preserve his body. His organs were replaced with aromatic herbs and he was washed from head to foot and wrapped in bandages. The young Tutankhamen was then taken to his hastily completed tomb, in a funeral procession that is shown on the cover of this book.

THE TOMB

The Egyptians believed that the dead traveled to a new life after death, so Tutankhamen was buried with many fine possessions that he would need in the next world. His tomb consisted of four rooms. The first room seen by Carter was the antechamber. This was filled with ornate carriages, furniture, and everyday items such as flyswatters and a wine strainer. The richest find here was a gold throne.

Two months later, after carefully recording the antechamber's contents, Carter opened the door to the main chamber. He found what seemed to be a wall of gold. It turned out to be the outer one of four golden shrines. Inside the shrines was a great stone sarcophagus.

COFFINS AND A CURSE

Under the granite lid of the stone sarcophagus were linen shrouds. These covered a life-size, gold-colored coffin made in the image of Tutankhamen. Inside were two more gold coffins. There was less than half an inch between the outer coffins, but in the tiny space were the remains of ancient flowers placed there by mourners over 3,000 years ago. In the third gold coffin was the mummy. Another 143 gold objects were found wrapped in the folds of the surrounding material, while on the mummy's face was a spectacular death mask (shown at the top of page 6). It was made of solid gold and set with lapis lazuli, a deep blue gemstone.

After the tomb was found, some people believed that Carter's expedition would be cursed for entering the sacred site. Indeed, the expedition's sponsor, Lord Carnarvon, died just six months later. He developed blood poisoning from an infected mosquito bite. It is said that at the moment of his death, all the lights in Cairo went out. In the years that followed, several other people who had connections with the tomb or expedition died unexpectedly or in unexplained circumstances, fueling rumors of the mummy's curse.

An eagle pendant was found in the tomb. The eagle was the royal symbol of ancient Egypt. The careful work shows the skill of the Egyptian craftsmen.

Inside the stone sarcophagus, Tutankhamen's mummified body was placed in three coffins. The outer two were made of wood covered in gold, but the final one was made from solid 22-carat gold.

outermost gold coffin

second gold coffin

third gold coffin

gold mask on mummy

7

The ruins of the Sumerian city of Ur lie in southern Iraq. Now just piles of rubble and the remains of some walls, 4,500 years ago Ur was one of the 14 great Sumerian city-states that flourished in this area.

Spectacular treasure finds in the royal tombs at Ur included gold statues of goats standing on their hind legs to nibble at a bush. These were possibly once the legs of a table.

Courtiers, servants, and guards take their drink of poison before they are entombed in one of the death pits at Ur.

EXCAVATIONS AT UR

Between 1922 and 1934 the archaeologist Sir Leonard Woolley excavated the site of Ur. In a huge cemetery he found 16 royal graves, each over 4,500 years old. Near some of the main chambers, bodies of courtiers, servants, and guards were found in large, deep pits. Woolley called one of these "The Great Death Pit" because it contained over 70 bodies.

A DRINK OF POISON

Beside each skeleton in the death pit was a little cup of metal or clay. The attendants and guards probably committed suicide by drinking poison from the cups after taking part in an elaborate funeral procession for the dead rulers. The bodies of those in the pit were then covered with earth.

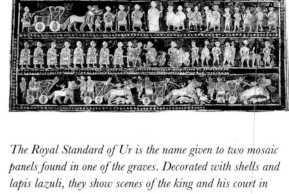

The Royal Standard of Ur is the name given to two mosaic panels found in one of the graves. Decorated with shells and lapis lazuli, they show scenes of the king and his court in times of peace and prosperity, as well as pictures of wars and battles.

QUEEN PU-ABI

In one of the main chambers the body of a woman, probably a queen, was found. Around her neck she wore a seal with her name, Pu-abi. Queen Pu-abi was buried wearing three elaborate headdresses. One was made with plain gold pendants, the second (shown at the top of the page) was of gold beech leaves, and the third was of long gold willow leaves with gold flowers. The upper part of her body was covered in beads of gold, silver, lapis lazuli, and other gemstones, which had perhaps once been sewn onto a cloak. She had gold rings on all her fingers, gold spiral earrings, and a garter of beads on her right knee. The bodies of two servants lay beside her.

BURIAL GOODS

Outside her burial chamber were the skeletons of five guards and a harpist whose finger bones were still in place on the instrument's strings. There were also 10 women with fine jewelry and headdresses similar to, but simpler than, the queen's. Two oxen, four grooms, and a sled on which they had perhaps pulled the Queen's body into the tomb, were nearby. Bowls of gold and silver and an ancient board game were among the many rich and interesting objects that lay among the skeletons.

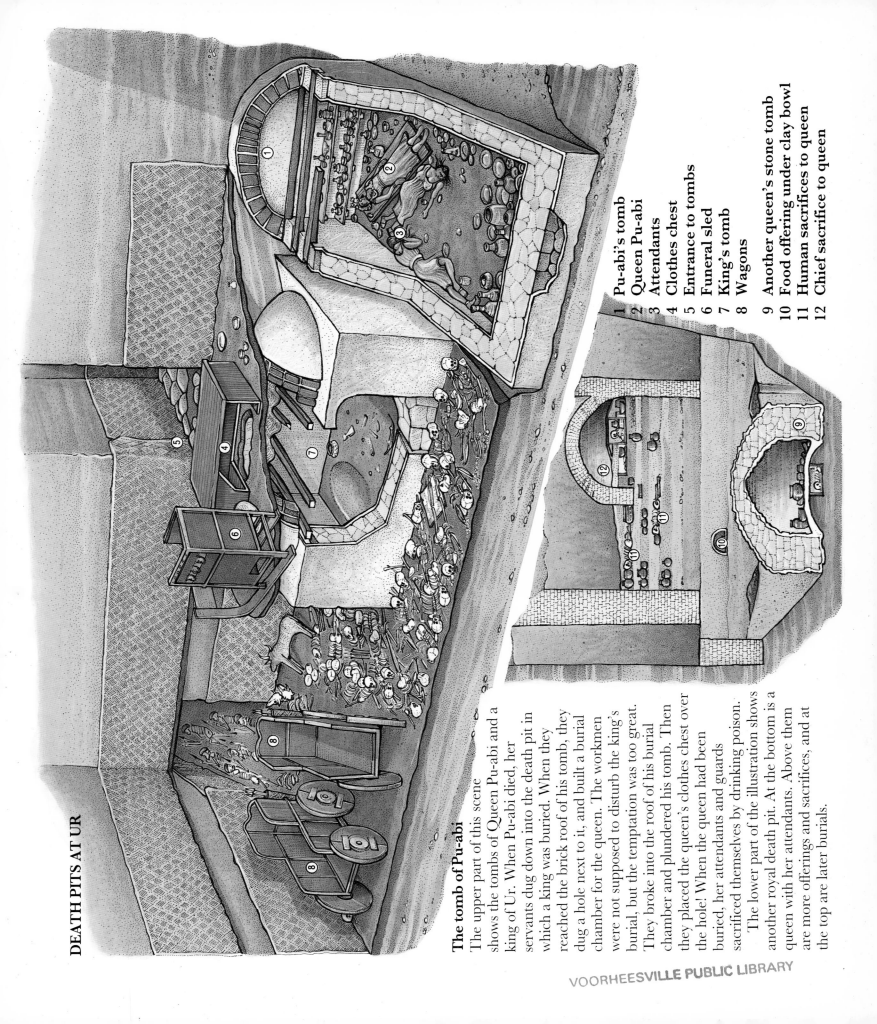

DEATH PITS AT UR

The tomb of Pu-abi

The upper part of this scene shows the tombs of Queen Pu-abi and a king of Ur. When Pu-abi died, her servants dug down into the death pit in which a king was buried. When they reached the brick roof of his tomb, they dug a hole next to it, and built a burial chamber for the queen. The workmen were not supposed to disturb the king's burial, but the temptation was too great. They broke into the roof of his burial chamber and plundered his tomb. Then they placed the queen's clothes chest over the hole! When the queen had been buried, her attendants and guards sacrificed themselves by drinking poison.

The lower part of the illustration shows another royal death pit. At the bottom is a queen with her attendants. Above them are more offerings and sacrifices, and at the top are later burials.

1 Pu-abi's tomb
2 Queen Pu-abi
3 Attendants
4 Clothes chest
5 Entrance to tombs
6 Funeral sled
7 King's tomb
8 Wagons
9 Another queen's stone tomb
10 Food offering under clay bowl
11 Human sacrifices to queen
12 Chief sacrifice to queen

VOORHEESVILLE PUBLIC LIBRARY

THE ETRUSCANS

A skillfully-crafted gold brooch, about 12 inches long, decorated with lions. The Etruscans loved rich jewelry.

When the Etruscans buried their dead, they clearly wanted to make them feel at home. Tombs of rich families often represented the inside of an Etruscan house—the walls were covered with carvings and paintings of everyday objects and activities from daily life.

THE ETRUSCANS

The Etruscans lived in city-states in what is now Tuscany, Italy. They were skillful sailors, warriors, merchants, and craftsmen, and were at the peak of their power around 600 to 500 B.C. The Etruscans are usually regarded as the ancestors of the Romans, by whom they were eventually conquered. One of the cities they controlled was Rome itself.

TOWNS OF TOMBS

The early Etruscan tombs were circular mounds, or tumuli, that contained burial chambers cut into the rock. Some of the largest measured up to 130 feet in diameter, housing many generations of the same family. Some mounds held more than one set of chambers, each with its own separate entrance.

The chambers of the tombs were often lavishly decorated. One, called the Tomb of the Reliefs, was decorated with reliefs (raised patterns carved on the walls) of weapons and household objects. Others showed characters from Greek mythology as well as scenes from everyday life.

The Etruscan cemeteries were laid out like towns, with avenues linked to each other. Wealthy families felt it was important to have impressive funeral rites and processions and elaborate tombs.

CEMETERIES

The Etruscans built cemeteries outside many of their cities. The cemetery near Caere (now Cerveteri in northern Italy) covered hundreds of acres. These sites were often laid out with avenues and squares and a main road along which the rich were taken to their final resting places. In one tomb a magnificent four-wheeled wagon has been found. It was probably used to carry the body of the warrior who was buried there.

The Etruscans often burned their dead in a special ceremony—called cremation—rather than burying them. They placed the ashes in containers in the tombs. These containers were made of terracotta or bronze, and shaped in the form of people, gods, houses, or even circular tombs.

BURIAL GOODS

The contents of the Etruscans' tombs have told us a great deal about their rituals, culture, and way of life. Finds include sculptures of the Etruscans and their gods made from bronze, stone, and terracotta, as well as bronze weapons and utensils and elaborate pieces of gold jewelry.

> **[The Etruscans have] tables sumptuously laid with everything that can contribute to delicate living; they have couch coverings embroidered with flowers and are served from quantities of silver dishes; and they have at their beck and call a considerable number of slaves.**
>
> *Posidonius*

A WEALTHY CITY

Many of the tombs have been plundered, but one found untouched near Caere in the early 19th century contained items made locally, goods imported from Greece, and some objects with motifs (patterns) from the Middle East. The discoveries in this tomb showed the great wealth of a noble Etruscan family—there were silver bowls, bronze shields, a full-size wooden chariot with bronze trimmings, gold necklaces, bracelets, and a gold brooch 12 inches long. Some historians believe that, in its time, Caere was the richest city in the world.

The Etruscans believed that the dead had the same needs as the living and furnished their tombs accordingly. In the Tomb of the Reliefs, objects from the daily life of a rich family are carved on the walls. There are pillows, linen and a linen chest, sandals, a wine jug, and a goose. The tomb dates from the fourth century B.C., and belonged to a wealthy Etruscan family.

11

High in the Altai mountains of Siberia, a Russian archaeologist saw some faint shapes through the ice. The only way he could think of to uncover these objects was to melt them out. So he boiled some water, poured it on the ice, and made his discoveries—frozen tombs!

A Scythian warrior has his arm tattooed. Some of the frozen bodies found in the tombs were so well preserved that they still had the tattoos on them.

FROZEN TOMBS

In 1947, the archaeologist, Sergei Rudenko, began to excavate one of the burial mounds in the remote valley of Pazyryk, Siberia. In this and in other frozen tombs he found ancient carpets from Persia, chariots from China, and horses wearing felt masks. All of these had belonged to the chieftains of an ancient nomadic people. Amazingly, he also found human bodies that still had tattoos on them, and grain in the stomachs of some of the buried horses.

This wonderful gold comb shows a horseman in Scythian dress fighting two attackers. Small objects like this could be carried by people who were always on the move.

THIEVES

Paradoxically, it was damage caused by thieves in the distant past that led to the preservation of the contents of these 2,300-year-old tombs. After the thieves broke in and left, water seeped in and then froze. Being underground, the ice was never melted by Siberia's brief summer sun.

The ice tombs date from the fifth century B.C., when parts of eastern Asia and the Middle East, and much of southeastern Europe, were controlled by nomadic horsemen known as the Scythians.

THE BURIALS

Until the discovery of their chieftains' tombs, the Scythians were only known from the accounts of ancient writers. The Greek historian Herodotus described how a Scythian leader was buried with goods and servants that he might need in another life after death. He also described how, a year after the burial, 50 of the finest men and horses were slain and placed on stakes around the burial mound, each rider sitting on his horse. Perhaps these horsemen were set around the tomb to guard the chieftain and his goods.

> **When they have laid the corpse upon a mattress in its chamber, they stick spears into the ground on all sides. Then they lay beams across and cover these with wicker, and bury one concubine, the cupbearer, a cook, a groom, an attendant, and a messenger.**
>
> *— Herodotus —*

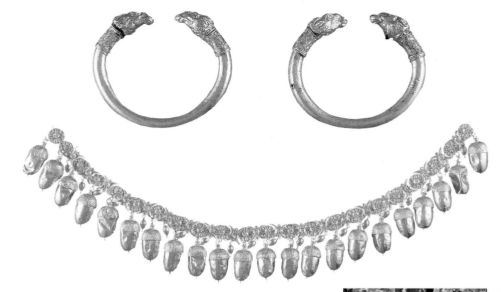

SCYTHIAN GOLD

Many tombs, like those at Pazyryk, were robbed of any gold they contained long ago, but some golden objects have survived at other sites. These works of art were decorated with horses or fashioned into the shapes of stags, bears, wolves, goats, eagles, and fish—wild animals that the Scythians would have seen around them.

Many of these gold items were made as decorations for bridles, but ornate swords, breast-plates, arrow quivers, and even combs of gold have also been found. All these valuable objects could easily be carried by nomadic people.

The frozen conditions of the ice tombs preserved many unique objects for nearly 2,500 years. Even this felt wall hanging of a horseman (above) has survived. There were no gold items found in the ice tombs in Siberia, but goldwork and jewelry like this gold necklace and these gold and bronze bracelets (top) have been found in other unlooted Scythian tombs.

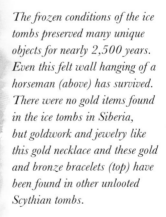

A reconstruction of the tomb of an early Scythian chieftain, based on excavations. He has been buried with members of his household and his horses. The tomb has been partly buried underground, with a mound of earth, called a barrow, raised above it.

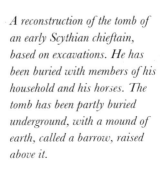

13

An enormous statue of a man in Carian dress is one of the very few pieces of the Mausoleum that still exist. It is believed to be Mausolus himself.

A chariot with four horses was carved out of marble for the top of Mausolus' tomb. On its base, this magnificent sculpture stood about twenty feet high.

The Mausoleum of the city of Halicarnassus was one of the Seven Wonders of the Ancient World. It ranked alongside the great pyramids of Egypt and the Hanging Gardens of Babylon. Today, only fragments of the Mausoleum exist.

MAUSOLUS

The Mausoleum at Halicarnassus was named after the man it was built for, Mausolus, the ruler of Caria in Asia Minor. The monument obviously made a great impression on anyone who saw it. By Roman times, 400 years later, the word mausoleum was used to describe any large tomb.

Ancient writers say that Mausolus' tomb was built by his wife Artemisia (who was also his sister) after his death in 353 B.C., although he probably ordered its construction himself.

THE RULER OF CARIA

In 377 B.C. Mausolus had become governor of Caria, part of the king of Persia's empire. In about 370 B.C. Mausolus moved the capital to Halicarnassus (now Bodrum in Turkey) and began to fill it with impressive buildings, many in Greek style. He wanted to encourage the spread of Greek art in Caria, and so the Mausoleum, too, was designed by Greek architects. He also arranged for the friezes to be sculpted by some of the most famous Greek sculptors of the time.

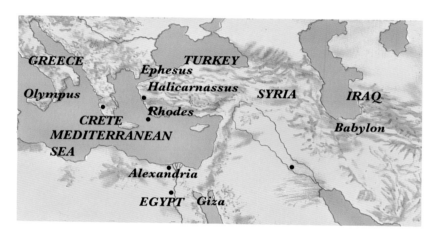

The ancient Greeks and Romans listed many objects that people should visit. The most commonly listed Seven Wonders of the Ancient World were the pyramids at Giza; the Temple of Artemis at Ephesus; the statue of Zeus at Olympus in Greece; the lighthouse of Alexandria harbor; the Colossus of Rhodes (a statue of the sun god Helios); the Hanging Gardens of Babylon; and the Mausoleum.

THE REMAINS

Unfortunately, an earthquake destroyed parts of the mausoleum in the 13th century. Later, many of the stones were reused in local buildings. Today just a few stones, statues, and fragments of the decorative friezes remain, so we can only speculate about what it actually looked like.

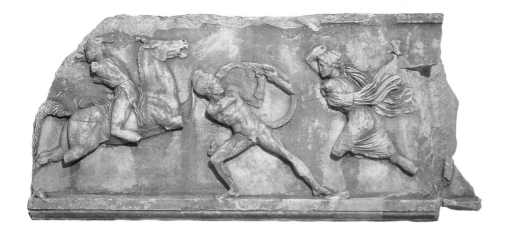

Part of the the Mausoleum's fame came from the elaborate carvings of the friezes around it. This piece shows a battle scene between Greeks and Amazons.

The Mausoleum was one of the major tourist sites of the ancient Mediterranean world. It stood above the harbor of Halicarnassus. We cannot be certain what it looked like. This illustration is based on ancient descriptions and the few remains that have survived.

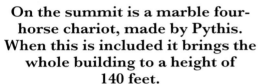

On the summit is a marble four-horse chariot, made by Pythis. When this is included it brings the whole building to a height of 140 feet.

Pliny the Elder

THE EVIDENCE

From the writings of Pliny the Elder and from the work of modern archaeologists, we know that the Mausoleum was rectangular, covering an area of about 115 feet by 100 feet, and it was probably about 130 feet high. The base was about 65 feet in height, on top of which were 36 columns. The roof was shaped like a pyramid, with 24 steps up to a platform on which stood a chariot with four horses. Possibly Mausolus himself was driving the chariot, like a god high above the Earth.

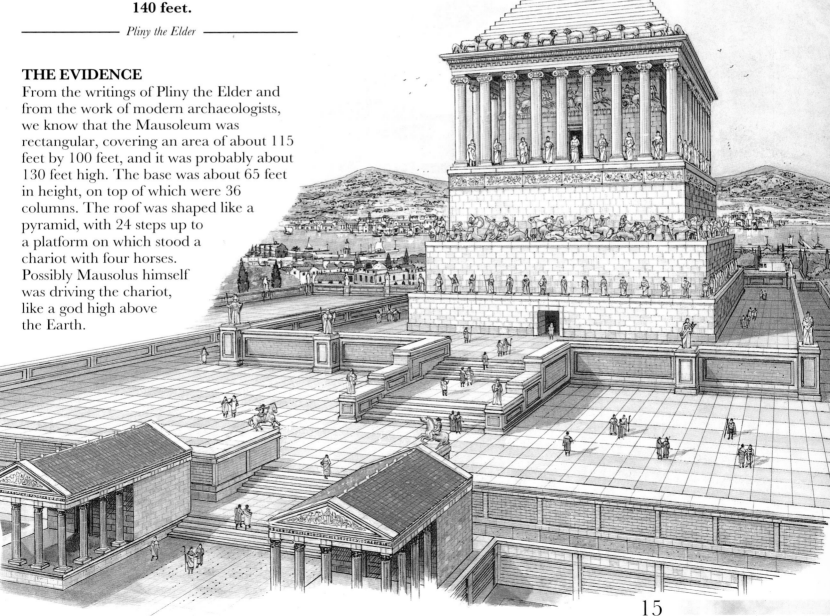

PHILIP OF MACEDONIA

An ivory bust of Philip, found in his tomb. After his assassination, Philip's body was partially cremated on a brick pyre (right) and the bones laid in a small gold casket, called a larnax. This was placed in his tomb, together with his gold oak wreath.

King Philip II of Macedonia was assassinated in 336 B.C. Philip, who had just conquered the Greek city-states and was about to attack the Persians, had many enemies. He may even have been killed by one of his own bodyguards.

A scene on the front of the tomb shows Philip out hunting with the royal pages. The mounted page on the left is possibly Philip's son Alexander the Great, who succeeded Philip and conquered a huge empire.

THE ROYAL TOMB
In 1977 excavations at the Macedonian capital of Aegae in northern Greece revealed what was obviously a royal tomb. Was it Philip's tomb? In the rear chamber of the tomb, the bones of a man in his forties were found in a small gold casket. Close examination showed that his eye socket and cheekbone had been badly damaged. Philip is known to have been hit by an arrow and blinded in one eye.

MORE CLUES
Rich grave goods in the king's chamber included a gold crown, silver cups, and bronze vessels, weapons, and armor. There were also some ivory heads—perhaps of Philip and his son Alexander—that had probably decorated a funeral couch. In the room outside, the antechamber, were a pair of leg greaves, armor made to protect the lower leg. One of these is shorter than the other, which is significant because we know Philip was lame. There was also a gold Scythian arrow case cover, and Philip is known to have campaigned in Scythian areas.

Also in the antechamber was another gold casket, containing the bones of a woman in her twenties, a purple robe, and a gold crown of flowers. This was probably one of the king's wives—maybe Cleopatra, who was murdered shortly after Philip's death. Based on these clues, archaeologists believe that the tomb is indeed Philip's.

MANY LAYERS

From the excavations, it seems that the Moche lords added new layers and maybe temples onto the first platform. Perhaps each lord wanted a bigger and more impressive temple than his predecessor.

THE SEE-THROUGH SCENE

The platform, temple, and position of the burials are shown in the see-through scene on the opposite page. Below is the richest burial, that of the Lord of Sipán and his attendants.

Moche craftworkers gilded many pieces of copperwork by dipping them in a chemical solution containing dissolved gold. The gold was then fixed in place by heating the piece.

Gilding a copper mask

1 **The Lord of Sipán**
2 **Wooden coffin**
3 **Guardian of the tomb**
4 **Young woman**
5 **Body of man with foot missing**
6 **Body of man with dog**
7 **Burial goods**

INVASION TREASURES

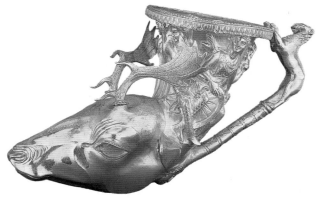

Treasures have always been hidden during invasions. Terrified people fleeing from their homes often hid their valuable possessions from the enemy. Sometimes the owners never returned, and their treasures lay undiscovered for many hundreds, even thousands, of years.

ROMAN TREASURE

Many hoards of treasures have been found throughout Europe in the areas that were once covered by the Roman Empire. One of the largest collections ever discovered is the Kaiserangst Hoard, which contained about 250 objects. These included coins, a magnificent silver table service, and a small silver statue of the goddess Venus looking at herself in a mirror. They were all found in a chest in the Kaiserangst fortress in Switzerland, once one of the biggest Roman strongholds on the Rhine-Danube frontier. It was probably abandoned during a tribal revolt.

THE MILDENHALL TREASURE

In 1942 a farmer in eastern England uncovered 34 pieces of Roman silver, an enormous dish that was over half a yard in diameter, and some spoons that were decorated with Christian symbols—the Mildenhall Treasure. This collection of silver probably belonged to a wealthy Roman family. It might have been buried to hide it from Saxon raiders, at the end of the fourth century A.D. This was a time when Britain was suffering attacks by Angles, Saxons, and Jutes from across the North Sea.

This beautiful gold rhyton was found near Panagyurishte. The rhyton was held high above the drinker's mouth while the liquid poured out of an opening in the animal's mouth.

VIKING RAIDS

In the ninth and tenth centuries, marauding pagan Vikings raided the coasts of Europe, plundering the villages and Christian monasteries. The monks tried to hide their valuables before they were captured or put to death. Often they took their secrets with them, never to return.

In 1980, several valuable items from early Christian times were discovered near the site of an old monastery at Derrynaflan in Ireland. A silver chalice, a bronze spoon, and a silver wafer dish were unearthed from a nearby peat bog. Had these been buried by a monk who heard the dreaded cry "The Vikings are coming"?

The large silver dish from the Mildenhall Treasure is over half a yard wide. At the center is a Roman god of the seas and rivers, Oceanus, surrounded by sea creatures. On the border are scenes of feasting presided over by Bacchus, the Roman god of wine.

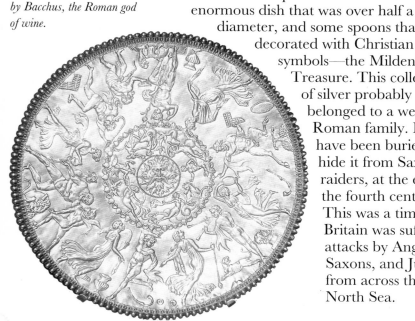

THRACIAN TREASURES

Many treasure finds have been made in the Balkans, where there have been numerous invasions and changes of rulers over the centuries. A spectacular discovery occurred in 1949 near the small town of Panagyurishte in central Bulgaria. Three laborers found nine incredible gold vessels including four drinking goblets, called rhytons, made in the shape of animals' heads.

The treasures were found on the site of an old Thracian settlement—the Thracians lived in Bulgaria from about 1000 B.C. These gold objects had been made by a skilled craftsman in Greece in about 330 B.C. Maybe a Thracian prince had commissioned them, or perhaps a powerful leader had accepted them as a bribe in return for his support. They were obviously buried in a time of crisis, and in a great hurry.

The Derrynaflan chalice, found in an Irish peat bog, is made of silver and decorated with golden scenes of animals and birds. It is set with 57 amber studs.

When the Vikings raided, the local people and monks rushed to hide their valuable possessions. The Vikings knew that Christian churches and monasteries often contained precious items of gold and silver.

THE TERRACOTTA ARMY

Farmers digging a well near the city of Xian in central China made an incredible discovery in 1974. Their tools struck an underground vault made of earth and timber. Inside they found thousands of life-size terracotta soldiers and horses.

THE FIRST EMPEROR

These clay sculptures were buried about a mile east of a great mound that covered the tomb of Shih Huang Ti, the first emperor of a united China. In 246 B.C. Shih Huang, at the age of 13, had become king of one of the many independent states in the region. Over the next few years he conquered the other states. When he founded his empire in 221 B.C. he centralized the government of China at his capital, which lay near present-day Xian.

THE DEATH OF SHIH HUANG

After a very active reign, Shih Huang died in 210 B.C. while journeying hundreds of miles from the capital. His adviser, Li Si, feared trouble within the empire if he could not return to the capital and secure the throne for one of Shih Huang's sons before the emperor's death was discovered. To keep the secret, Li Si delivered food to the emperor's covered chariot, and issued decrees in his name. Li Si even had fish placed in each carriage of the procession to cover the smell of the decaying corpse. Although Li Si succeeded in crowning Shih Huang's heir, the new emperor was soon killed in a revolt.

When Emperor Shih Huang died, his chief adviser covered up the death. He arranged for the imperial carriage to return to the capital as if nothing had happened. The people who saw it pass probably had no idea there was a dead body inside. Those that did guess were too afraid to reveal the secret.

28

SHIH HUANG'S TOMB

As soon as Shih Huang had become king of his own state he had ordered work to begin on his tomb. When he became emperor of China his plans grew even more ambitious. We know from the writings of a Chinese historian that it took 700,000 men 36 years to build his tomb. It was said to be like an underground city, with a throne room and treasure house, as well as walls, gates, and a watchtower.

To keep its contents secret, many of the workmen were killed and buried within the tomb. Even today, archaeologists have not excavated it, partly because of dangerous booby-traps put there to prevent thieves from stealing the treasure.

THE TERRACOTTA ARMY

There are no records of the amazing 10,000-man terracotta army, though it is believed that the figures were made to guard the emperor's tomb. Three vaults have now been discovered. The largest, measuring almost 700 feet by 200 feet, contains 6,000 figures in battle formation. This is an infantry regiment with a vanguard (leading unit) of unarmored archers. The second vault contains units of cavalry and chariots, while the third, with 68 figures and a wooden chariot, is probably the terracotta army's command headquarters.

THE FIGURES

The men were buried with real bows, swords, spears, and crossbows. Traces of color show that the soldiers' clothes were once painted bright yellow, purple, and green. The faces of all the terracotta warriors are different and it has been suggested that they are copied from the real members of the emperor's army who allowed themselves to be sculpted rather than be buried alive. Some faces show the different racial features of people from the farthest borders of the Chinese empire that Shih Huang had created.

The various military ranks of the terracotta army had different hairstyles and headdresses. A general's (right) was the most eleborate of those shown here. The back of his cap was tied into a bow. Other officers and charioteers wore bonnets or caps (center). The infantry (left) did not have caps and had their hair coiled in a topknot.

The 10,000 terracotta warriors stood in battle formation, ready to defend the tomb of the emperor from any attack. Most of the army was comprised of footsoldiers (left). There was also a group of officers and a chariot (below).

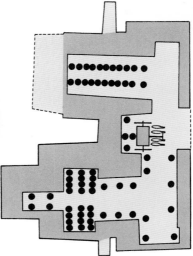

THE TOMB OF PACAL

Many of the buildings in Pacal's great city of Palenque were decorated with carvings. This one of a Mayan god was found on a palace.

After three years of painstaking work, the Mexican archaeologist Alberto Ruz and his colleagues finally reached a rich tomb underneath the temple they were excavating. It contained the skeleton of a man whose face was covered by an amazing mask made from over 200 pieces of jade—Pacal the Great, once the powerful ruler of the Mayan city of Palenque.

THE DISCOVERY

At the start of the excavations, Alberto Ruz noticed that one of the stone slabs on the floor of a temple called the Temple of Inscriptions had some holes in it. Ruz wondered if the holes had been made so that the slab could be lifted with ropes. Realizing that the temple wall did not stop at floor level, he started to dig.

Under the floor he found steps and a secret passage leading down for 80 feet. It took three years to work carefully through the rubble that filled the passage. Finally, in 1952 he found a small box of jade, shells, and pottery between two walls that crossed the passage; behind the second wall he found a larger box. This contained the skeletons of six young humans who had probably been sacrificed by the temple's priests.

The carvings on the slab covering Pacal's tomb are impressive. The dead king is depicted falling into the Underworld. From the center of his body grows the Maya "World Tree" with a large heavenly bird on top. This symbolizes that on his death the king became a god.

PACAL THE GREAT

Next Ruz found a great triangular slab blocking the end of the corridor, and behind it an enormous room. The walls of this room were covered in carvings, and in the center lay a large rectangular stone slab. Beneath this engraved slab lay Pacal in his jade mask.

Pacal also had jade discs on his ears, jade bead necklaces, and jade rings on his fingers. He held a piece of jade in each hand and another had been placed in his mouth. Two jade figures, one representing the Sun God, lay beside him.

Pacal's body was dressed in many jade ornaments, including this jade necklace.

JADE

The use of jade in Pacal's burial makes a fascinating comparison with the practices of the ancient Chinese, who believed that a dead body should be buried with jade to preserve it. Pacal's mask was made of jade collected from a wide area. The Maya, who were at the height of their power in Central America from about A.D. 300 to 800, traded their pottery, jade, and other goods throughout the region. They built large cities with palaces and temples, where they carried out great ceremonies, including human sacrifices.

THE RULER OF PALENQUE

Pacal ruled Palenque from A.D. 613 to 683. During his reign, one of the many buildings he constructed was the Temple of the Inscriptions, under which his tomb lies. The building work was continued by his two successors. By A.D. 720, Palenque had grown from a minor ceremonial center to a powerful city.

Pacal's tomb was found deep below the Temple of the Inscriptions. Many sacrifices and other ritual celebrations were carried out in the temple and on its steps. These celebrations played an important part in the lives of the Mayan people.

SUTTON HOO

This is one of two ornate shoulder clasps found in the ship at Sutton Hoo. They probably once fastened part of the king's armor.

In May 1939, as war was breaking out in Europe, a local archaeologist, Basil Brown, was at work on a site on the southeast coast of England. On the grounds of an estate named Sutton Hoo he discovered fragments of items from mounds and barrows. Had this once been an important burial site?

THE SHIP

Brown began work on the largest of 16 burial mounds, which was about 90 feet long and almost 10 feet high, with the help of the estate's gardeners. Over the next few days they began to uncover the outlines of an enormous ship. The planks had decayed long before, but the sand was slightly discolored where the wood and rusty iron rivets had once been joined together. There were signs that the mound had been broken into in the late 16th or early 17th century, but the chamber in the center seemed to be undisturbed.

The ship was probably rowed along the coast and then pulled up from the estuary shore to its final resting place. Although this is now half a mile inland, it was probably only about 650 yards from the water in the seventh century. Hoo means "spur of land" and the ship was buried on what was once a small promontory. A tent-shaped funeral chamber was probably specially built onto the ship once it was in position.

> There in the harbor stood
> the ring-powered ship,
> The prince's vessel, shrouded in
> ice and eager to sail;
> And then they laid their lord,
> the giver of the rings, deep
> within the ship
> By the mast in majesty; many
> treasures
> And adornments from far and
> wide were gathered there.
>
> —— *Beowulf* ——

At this point a team of professional archaeologists took over the dig. Inside the chamber they found an amazing variety of items that dated from the sixth and seventh centuries, and indicated that the burial was in honor of an Anglo-Saxon king. There were no traces of a body, however. It may be that the ship was intended as a memorial, not a grave.

THE ANGLO-SAXONS

The Angles and the Saxons had journeyed across the North Sea from Germany and Denmark as the Romans left Britain in the fifth century A.D. Little is known about their early years in England, so the contents of the Sutton Hoo ship, which was buried in the old Anglo-Saxon kingdom of East Anglia, have provided valuable evidence of their way of life.

Inside the burial chamber many items reflected the wealth of this ruler and his peoples' trading contacts. He had an ornate helmet decorated with iron and bronze creatures, and a shield. Both are thought to have come from Sweden. There was also a highly decorated gold buckle that, although made in England, is in a traditional Swedish style; coins from France; silver bowls, cups, and spoons from Greece; and a bronze bowl from the Near East. A great silver dish bearing the name of the Byzantine emperor Anastasius (A.D. 491-518) was also found. There were also drinking horns, a lyre, an iron lamp filled with beeswax, bonehandled knives, combs, leather shoes, the remains of fine clothes, and many other objects that would have been useful for the king's next life.

WHO WAS THE KING?

But who was the king? Two small silver spoons with Christian symbols give us a clue. They are strange items to find in a pagan burial, and suggest that the ship was in honor of Raedwald, a powerful king of East Anglia who died about A.D. 625. He is known to have received missionaries and converted to Christianity for a while.

A purse buried in the ship contained 37 gold coins, each from a different part of France. The leather pouch had rotted away, and only the lid survives. The lid is set with garnets, emeralds, and pieces of gold.

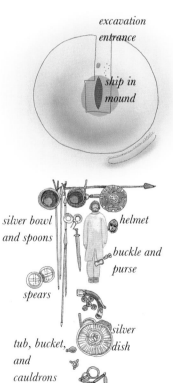

The items were laid out in the tomb as if a body had been there. Did it disintegrate, or was there never a body?

33

TAMERLANE

When the great Mongol emperor Tamerlane died on February 18, 1405, his advisers kept his death a secret. His body was scented with rose water, musk, and camphor and returned to his central Asian capital, Samarkand, without anyone else knowing.

TAMERLANE'S DEATH

These precautions were necessary so that Tamerlane's chosen heir would have time to return to Samarkand and secure his own rule of the empire before news of the death broke.

Most of the princes who might have wished to take over the large empire were refused entry to the city. Only a small number were allowed in to pay their respects to the former emperor and to accompany his widows and some of the princesses in mourning.

Tamerlane observes the building of his mausoleum. Ironically, he probably built it for a grandson rather than for himself. The grandson died in 1403, but when Tamerlane died two years later his body was put there, too.

GUR-I AMIR

Tamerlane's tomb, which is part of a funeral complex called the Gur-i Amir (the Lord's Tomb), may have been meant for one of his grandsons, who died in 1403. However, Tamerlane's body was also laid to rest there, in 1405, and it was later used to bury some of his descendents as well.

In addition to the towering tomb, the complex included a madrassa (a college for religious studies) and a caravanserai (an inn for travelers).

TIMUR THE LAME

Tamerlane's real name was Timur. Tamerlane, the name by which he is best known, means Timur-the-lame. When his tomb was opened by Russian archaeologists in 1941, they found the skeleton of a man who was deformed in both the limbs on his right-hand side.

A MAJESTIC TOMB

The tomb itself is octagonal, with a high round drum rising upward. On top of this is a large ribbed dome with beautiful turquoise tiles. Inside, the tomb is decorated with patterns of gold, red, and blue, and on the ceiling there are designs in gold and blue papier-mâché.

On the coffin of Tamerlane is a large slab of jade. This was brought back from a campaign in the northeast in 1424–25 by his grandson, Ulugh-Beg. He had the jade inscribed to show Tamerlane's family line traced back to a mythical Mongol queen whose descendents included Gengis Khan, the first great Mongol emperor.

Tamerlane used terrifying tactics to beat his opponents. His men made towers from the heads of his slaughtered enemies outside cities he wished to frighten into surrender.

Then . . . we found Timur . . . He was sitting on the ground, but upon a raised dais before which there was a fountain that threw up a column of water into the air backward, and in the basin of the fountain there were floating red apples.

—————— *Spanish ambassador* ——————

TAMERLANE THE GREAT

So what was the man who had ordered the building of this splendid tomb like? Tamerlane had a reputation for being very cruel to his enemies, yet he was also described as a cultured man who developed a court where art and writing proclaimed both the Islamic faith and the success of his great empire.

Tamerlane had been a chieftain in one of the states that succeeded the powerful Mongol empire of Gengis Khan. In the 1360s Tamerlane began brutal new conquests, which eventually stretched from India across Russia and to the Mediterranean Sea. As he conquered lands, Tamerlane took the finest artists and craftworkers he could find to his capital of Samarkand. He himself spent little time in Samarkand because he was often away on military campaigns. The Gur-i Amir was among the many buildings constructed by these craftsmen.

Tamerlane sits on a throne during celebrations near his capital of Samarkand. He took artists and scholars from the lands he conquered to make his court a place of learning and culture.

SPANISH TREASURE

Pieces of eight, or ocho reales, were Spanish coins made from the plentiful silver found in the Americas. They were popular booty for pirates because they were used in many parts of the world and could be divided easily.

I n the 16th century, Spanish adventurers conquered the enormous empires of the Incas and Aztecs. There they found amazing riches—gold, silver, and other valuable treasures—which they plundered ruthlessly. They melted down many of the Indians' ornate ceremonial objects and took the precious metals back to Spain.

TREASURE MINES

When these riches began to run out, the Spanish started to organize the mining of gold and silver. One of the largest silver mines was at Potosí in modern Bolivia. A century later, in 1660, it was calculated that enough silver had been mined there to build a 50-foot-wide road from Potosí to the Spanish capital of Madrid.

Each year two fleets would take supplies and trading goods from Spain out to the Americas. There they would fill the ships until they were laden with treasure. To deter pirates and privateers on the return journey, the treasure ships would gather into great fleets at the port of Havana and set out for home under the protection of armed galleons.

PRIVATEERS

The privateers were sailors on armed ships who were allowed by their governments to seize the cargo of "enemy" vessels. Sir Francis Drake, an Englishman, was one. He captured over 100 Spanish ships, including the *Nuestra Señora de la Conçepcion*, which had 90 pounds of gold bars, 28 tons of silver, and 13 chests of coins on board at the time. He was knighted for his exploits in 1580 by Queen Elizabeth I.

HURRICANES

Hurricanes were another great threat to the treasure fleets. On the return journey from Havana to Spain, the treasure fleets tried to avoid the late summer hurricanes in the Caribbean. They aimed to set sail from the Americas before the end of June. Sometimes the loading took longer than expected, and often the delayed ships were caught, and sank, in bad storms.

Many treasure finds have come from Spanish ships lost in storms. This painting shows a ship battling its way home through heavy seas.

Every year two Spanish fleets would sail to the Americas with supplies and trading goods. They would then be loaded for the return journey with every type of treasure and goods imaginable, from silver and pearls to sugar and dyes. Often ships were severely overloaded in an effort to cram everything in — which made them more likely to capsize in storms.

THE 1715 FLEET

By 1715 no treasure ships had sailed for a while because of wars between Spain and England, so that year's fleet was even more heavily laden than usual. When the ships left Havana late in July, they were driven by a hurricane onto the reefs of the Florida Keys, and over a thousand people drowned.

In the 1940s a blackened coin, dated 1714, was found on a beach near Kennedy Space Center in Florida and eventually led to the discovery of many of the ships of the 1715 fleet. The cargo retrieved included gold chains, jewelry, silver plate, and a chest full of 3,000 silver coins called *ocho reales*, the famous Spanish "pieces of eight."

All these items were found on the shipwrecked Nuestra Senõra de las Maravillas. *Alongside gold bars and coins were items of personal jewelry such as gold chains and rings with valuable gemstones.*

TREASURE GALORE

There were many other wrecks of treasure ships lost in hurricanes in the Caribbean. From one great ship lost in 1622, silver bars worth nearly $375 million were recovered. Despite their losses, the Spanish treasure fleets had done their work—over 30 million pounds of silver were taken back to Spain, and relatively little of it was lost at sea to pirates, privateers, or hurricanes.

EL DORADO

This gold model probably shows the raft used in the El Dorado ceremony. It was found in a cave near Lake Guatavita.

The new leader was covered in gold dust and then rowed onto the lake. When the raft reached the middle, the crowds stopped singing, and gold and other precious objects were thrown into the water.

For four centuries the words El Dorado have been linked with myths of fabulous amounts of undiscovered gold treasure. "El Dorado" literally means "The Golden Man" in Spanish. It originally referred to an Indian warrior who, the Spaniards believed, ruled a great golden city.

THE STORY

The stories of El Dorado reached western Europe in the 16th century when the Spanish invaded South America. Many treasure seekers were tempted to search for the city. They believed it was hidden deep in the rainforests or high on a mountain plateau, and their expeditions went far into unexplored regions.

LAKE GUATAVITA

The story of the gold seems to have arisen from a ceremony performed by a people known as the Chibcha, or Muisca. They lived by Lake Guatavita in the northern Andes, in what is now Colombia.

The lake was sacred to them. They believed that they had to make offerings of gold and other precious objects to appease a demon-god who lived in the lake. Whenever the Chibcha had a new leader they would cover him in gold dust. Then he would be placed on a raft alongside four of his chieftains and rowed out into the lake.

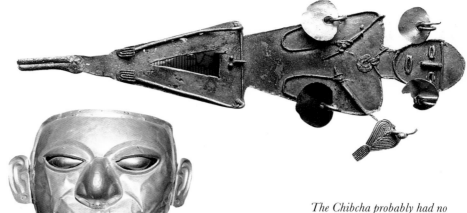

At this time they stripped the heir to his skin and annointed him with a sticky earth on which they placed gold dust so that he was completely covered with this metal.

— *Juan Rodríguez Freyle* —

As the raft left the shore, the Chibcha played music with trumpets, flutes, and other instruments, and started singing. The sound was deafening, until the raft reached the center of the lagoon, when they raised a banner as a signal for silence. The "golden man" and his companions then made their offerings.

TREASURE HUNTING SCHEMES

The reports of this ceremony have inspired many people to search for the gold treasure. The first person to try to drain Lake Guatavita was Hernán Pérez de Quesada. In 1544 he organized local Indians into a long human chain and made them tip out the water with empty gourds. After more than three months of work the water level of the lake had dropped by ten feet, and several valuable items were found along its edge.

The next major scheme was undertaken in 1578 when Don Antonio Sepúlveda had a channel cut into the surrounding rock by 8,000 native Indians. As the water flowed out of the lake, it revealed some objects lying on the 60 feet of newly exposed mud. According to a witness, these included "serpents, eagles, a staff covered with gold plaques and hung with little gold tubes, and an emerald the size of a hen's egg."

AN ANGRY GOD

Sepúlveda then ordered work on the channel to continue, but when the sides of it collapsed, killing hundreds of workers, the men refused to carry on. They believed this was a sign from the angry demon-god of the lake.

FINAL ATTEMPTS

Since Sepúlveda's channel there have been many expeditions whose aim was to extract the treasure from the lake, or to find El Dorado elsewhere in South America. These have included several ambitious schemes this century, using modern technology.

However, no one has ever successfully drained or dredged the center of Lake Guatavita, and probably no one ever will. In 1965 the Colombian government made the lake a national reserve and outlawed any further salvage attempts.

The Chibcha probably had no source of gold on their own lands. They often made their jewelry and figures flat to get the best effect from what they could obtain by trading. Finely crafted pieces like these were probably thrown into Lake Guatavita during the ceremony.

This illustration from a Spanish manuscript shows Indians panning a stream for gold. They regarded gold as a valuable commodity and made it into beautiful sacred objects.

39

THE *MARY ROSE*

This is the only known picture of the Mary Rose *from the 16th century. It is in a list of Henry VIII's ships known as the Anthony Roll, completed in 1546. We know from the research and survey of the wreck that the picture is not very accurate.*

One calm summer day in July 1545, King Henry VIII of England was watching his navy engage a large French invasion fleet. Standing on the shore at Portsmouth, the king looked on in horror as his favorite warship, the *Mary Rose*, keeled over and sank before his eyes.

CONSTRUCTION

Soon after he came to the English throne in 1509, Henry VIII began to strengthen the English navy. The 700-ton *Mary Rose* was constructed in Portsmouth in 1509–10. It was made almost entirely from oak and had a keel (backbone) over 100 feet long. In 1545 it is known to have carried 39 heavy iron and bronze cannons, as well as 30 lighter breech-loading swivel cannons.

A SUCCESSFUL SHIP

For 35 years the *Mary Rose* was a successful warship, the pride of the fleet. In a letter to King Henry in 1513, Sir Edward Howard described it as "Your good ship, the flower I trow of all ships that ever sailed." But on that fateful day, the ship's captain fired one broadside at the enemy's war galleys, then turned the ship tightly so the guns on the other side could fire. As the ship "went about," water rushed into the gun ports that were open and ready for action. This caused a sudden loss of stability and the ship capsized. As many as 700 soldiers and sailors went down with the *Mary Rose*, and less than 40 of the crew survived.

A large chest was found inside the ship's surgeon's cabin, containing bowls, ointment cans, and metal syringes. The cabin's ceiling was only a little over five feet high. In this tiny room the surgeon had to deal with the casualties of battle and infectious diseases.

THE WRECK

Almost immediately, the navy tried to raise the ship by lifting it by the masts. The attempt was unsuccessful, and the operation was abandoned. The ship stayed on the seabed, under 40 feet of water, for another 400 years, until the site was discovered by divers in 1970.

I trust by Monday or Tuesday at the furthest the *Mary Rose* shall be weighted [raised] up and saved. There be two hulkes, cables, pulleys and other things made up for weighing her.

— *Charles Brandon* —

The divers found that a build-up of silt had preserved much of the starboard (right) side of the hull as well as over 20,000 items from the ship. After preparations were made for a very careful salvage operation, the surviving side of the hull was raised and towed into Portsmouth harbor in 1982. The ship and its contents are like a time capsule of life in the 16th century.

A bronze muzzle-loading gun salvaged from the Mary Rose. *The elm carriage could be pulled back for cleaning and reloading the barrel.*

THE *MARY ROSE*

20,000 treasures

After the *Mary Rose* was salvaged, an inventory of the ship revealed thousands of items of both everyday and military life, including navigational equipment and weapons (3,500 arrows and 138 whole longbows were found), as well as personal items. The latter included leather covers of books and silk embroidered purses. Over 60 objects from the ship's surgeon's kit survived, including cans of ointments, peppercorns, and also three metal syringes, while a bag of leather shoes awaiting repair showed that a cobbler was on hand to repair old shoes.

1 Sterncastle
2 Hold
3 Galley (kitchen)
4 Step for main mast
5 Oak timbers
6 Keel of elm
7 Cross-timbers ("riders") added for strength
8 Iron breech-loading gun
9 Bronze muzzle-loading gun
10 Main deck
11 Barber surgeon's cabin
12 Forecastle

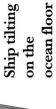

Ship tilting on the ocean floor

Longbows and arrows

PRESERVED BODIES

This 500-year old Eskimo child was found in a cave in Greenland. Its body and clothing were preserved by the cold.

The body of Lindow Man was preserved by the conditions of a peat bog. Lack of air delayed decomposition while chemicals in the peat turned the skin into leather.

In August 1984, part of a human leg was found in a peat bog in Lindow Moss, England. The police were called in and also the county archaeologist. Was this a recent murder victim or an ancient corpse?

THE BODY IN THE BOG
The rest of the body from the waist up was soon located. Although it had been flattened by the weight of the surrounding peat, it was remarkably well preserved. Radiocarbon tests revealed that the body, now called Lindow Man, was over 2,000 years old!

CLUES TO AN ELUSIVE IDENTITY
Dental examinations showed that Lindow Man was about 25–30 years old when he died. His fingernails were surprisingly smooth and manicured, indicating that he had not done a lot of heavy work and probably wasn't a laborer, farmer, or craftsman. He was healthy and in good physical condition, and had reddish-brown hair, a mustache, and a beard.

Bodies are sometimes preserved by very hot, dry conditions. This skeleton was found in the dry desert of coastal Peru.

A HUMAN SACRIFICE?
But what had caused Lindow Man's death? Further research showed that Lindow Man had been murdered. His skull was fractured, possibly by blows from a heavy ax. He had also been strangled by a cord that was still tightly knotted around his neck. Because of his unusual injuries, some scientists believe that he was killed as part of a ritual. One theory suggests that Lindow Man was a Druid, or Celtic priest, who was sacrificed to the gods to protect the Celts from a Roman invasion.

BOG CONDITIONS
The special conditions found in bogs have preserved many bodies. Bogs are very watery yet do not contain much air, so there are no bacteria to break down the bodies. In Denmark over 150 bodies have been found in bogs, in Germany over 200, in Holland about 50, and in the British Isles at least 120. Many bodies have also been found in North American bogs, some of them buried in simple graves.

SPECIAL CLIMATES
Bog conditions are not the only ones that can prevent decay. So, too, can the dry desert climates of the southwestern United States, China, and Peru. Icy temperatures in the Arctic Circle and on high mountaintops have also preserved bodies.

 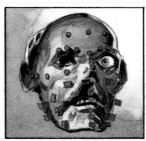  

A reconstruction of Ötzi's face was made to show how he might have looked (left). Using computer information and measurements of the amount of flesh and muscle on living people, modeling plastic was added to a copy of the skull. Pegs were used to show when the correct depth of "flesh" amd "muscle" had been added. Ötzi might have been on a hunting trip, or perhaps making a long journey (below).

THE ALPINE ICE MAN

In September 1991 a German couple hiking in the Alps near the Austrian-Italian border saw a head and shoulders jutting out of the ice. At first it was thought to be the body of a missing 20th century climber. But radiocarbon tests showed that he was 5,000 years old.

The man has been called Ötzi, after the Ötztal valley near where he died. Ötzi was found high up in the mountains at over 10,000 feet. His body survived the movements of a nearby glacier because it was protected by a rocky hollow.

ÖTZI'S BELONGINGS

Ötzi was carrying a copper ax, a dagger with a flint blade, a deerskin quiver with 14 arrows, and a six-foot-long bow. Remains of a backpack built around a wooden frame were found, and his clothes were made of leather and packed with grass for insulation. Ötzi had tattoos on his back, knees, and ankles. Around his neck he wore a leather necklace with a stone bead. He also had a piece of fungus on a string, which may have been a kind of medicine. Or perhaps the tattoos, the stone, and the fungus had some spiritual significance. Again, we can only guess.

Ötzi's ax had a copper blade bound to a wooden handle. It is the oldest ax ever found in Europe with bindings and a handle.

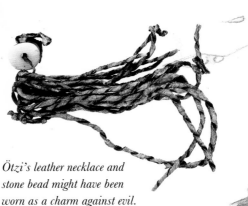

Ötzi's leather necklace and stone bead might have been worn as a charm against evil.

THE TAJ MAHAL

Above is a picture of Mumtaz Mahal, for whom the mausoleum was built. Her beauty was legendary. The moon, court poets said, hid its face in shame before her because she was so beautiful.

Mumtaz Mahal, the favorite wife of Mogul emperor Shah Jahan, died shortly after giving birth to her fourteenth baby in 1631. Legend says that as she lay dying she whispered to her husband, "Build a monument that will symbolize our love forever."

MOURNING
After her death, Shah Jahan ordered the whole country to go into mourning for two years. All music, brightly colored clothes, jewelry, and perfume were banned. He was so faithful to his wife's wish that he asked architects to submit plans for a mausoleum for her. No one knows who the architect was, but work began on the Taj Mahal in 1632.

THE BUILDING
The Taj Mahal was built just outside Shah Jahan's capital of Agra, which is on the Yamuna (Jumna) River in northern India. Over 20,000 workmen took 22 years building the Taj Mahal complex. The mausoleum alone took 10 years to complete. The Taj was named after Mumtaz, whose name means "Chosen of the Palace."

> **[The builders used] blocks of marble...
> of such unusual size and length that
> they drew the sweat of many powerful
> teams of oxen and fierce-looking,
> big-horned buffaloes...dragging
> enormous, strongly-made wagons.**
>
> *— Sebastian Manrique —*

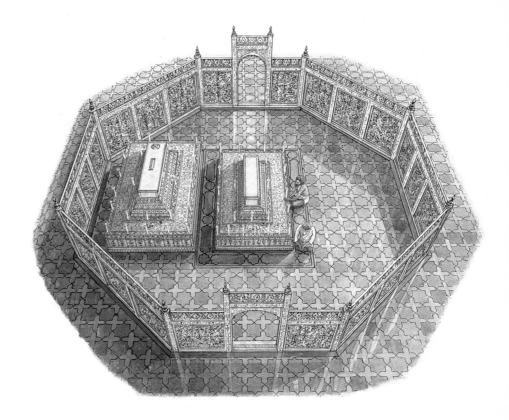

A GRAND LAYOUT

Like earlier Mogul tombs, the Taj Mahal is not just one building but a series of structures, walls, and gardens. It is laid out in a rectangle running from north to south and covers an area measuring 1,900 by 1,000 feet. The mausoleum itself is made of white marble, which takes on different colors in different lights. Facing one side of the mausoleum is a mosque made of red sandstone with a marble dome. To balance this, its *jawab*, or "answer," stands on the other side. There are also stables and rooms for guards in the complex.

THE MEMORIALS

Mumtaz's marble memorial lies in the center of the mausoleum, with her husband's beside her. The actual tombs are in a chamber below this room. Shah Jahan's memorial tomb is the only part of the whole Taj Mahal complex that is not perfectly symmetrical. This arrangement supports the theory that perhaps Shah Jahan planned a similar black Taj for himself across the river.

The memorial tombs of Mumtaz Mahal and Shah Jahan lie close to each other in the center of the Taj Mahal's mausoleum. A finely-carved marble screen studded with precious stones surrounds them.

The Taj Mahal (far left), showing the mosque and its jawab, or "answer." Craftsmen came from all over India and Asia to build it. The Taj is decorated with beautiful carvings and fine inlays. Flowers (left) are Islamic symbols of the rewards that the faithful will find in paradise.

45

KEY DATES AND GLOSSARY

Many of the early dates given here are approximate because precise records of the events do not exist. The first major tombs appear about 2,500 B.C., when people first began to live in cities. Because wealth was often concentrated in these areas, rulers could afford to build enormous tombs and have them filled with precious treasures.

B.C.

c.3,000	Ötzi, the Alpine Ice Man, dies
2,630	First pyramid begun in Egypt
c.2,500	Royal graves at Ur
1323	Tutankhamen buried
c.600-500	Etruscans at height of their power in Tuscany, Italy
c.500	Scythian horsemen in southeastern Europe, the Middle East, and Asia
353	Mausolus of Halicarnassus dies
336	Philip II of Macedonia is assassinated
210	Emperor Shih Huang dies
206	Han dynasty founded in China
113	Han prince Liu Sheng dies
c.50	Lindow Man is killed

A.D.

79	Mount Vesuvius buries Pompeii
625	King Raedwald of East Anglia dies, and perhaps is buried in the Sutton Hoo ship
683	Pacal, Maya ruler of Palenque, dies
1405	Tamerlane dies
1544	First attempt to drain Lake Guatavita in Colombia
1632	Work begins on the Taj Mahal
1545	The *Mary Rose* sinks
1733	Ships of one of the last Spanish treasure fleets are wrecked in a hurricane in the Caribbean

Finding treasure

Most countries in the world have laws concerning the discovery of treasure and other artifacts. If you find gold, silver, something precious, or just something that seems old, you should immediately report it to the local authorities and the land's owner. This does not mean you will have to hand over the object. Depending on what you have found, you may be able to keep it or be given a reward. Don't trespass on private property, and never search on an archaeological site unless you are part of an authorized excavation team.

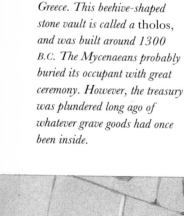

The Treasury of Atreus is the most impressive of many Mycenaean tombs found in Greece. This beehive-shaped stone vault is called a tholos, and was built around 1300 B.C. The Mycenaeans probably buried its occupant with great ceremony. However, the treasury was plundered long ago of whatever grave goods had once been inside.

Glossary

barrow: a mound of earth placed over a tomb, often surrounded by a ditch.

dolmen: an ancient stone construction thought to be a tomb. Several vertical stones support a horizontal stone.

mausoleum: a large elaborate tomb. Named after the enormous and splendid tomb built for Mausolus, king of Caria in the fourth century.

mosque: a Muslim place of worship

mummification: the process of preserving or embalming a body for burial, especially practiced in ancient Egypt.

pieces of eight: Spanish coins worth eight *reales*. A *real* was a small Spanish silver coin. Pirates preferred coins as booty because they were easy to divide into shares.

radiocarbon dating: a technique for finding out the age of organic materials, like bodies.

sarcophagus: a stone coffin or tomb, often with inscriptions or sculptures.

shroud: a garment or piece of cloth used to wrap up a dead body.

Quotations

The quotations in this book come from a variety of sources. Many of them were written long after the events they describe, but some are the accounts of eyewitnesses, such as the description of Tamerlane's court by the Spanish Ambassador in the 14th century.

Posidonius (c.135–c.51 B.C.) was a Greek philosopher, scientist, and writer, born in Syria. Herodotus (c.485–425 B.C.) was a Greek historian who wrote about the wars between the Greeks and their neighbors, such as the Scythians. He was born in Halicarnassus. Pliny the Elder (A.D. 23–79) was a Roman military commander and later a writer. The description of the Mausoleum of Halicarnassus comes from his *Natural History* (XXXVI, 30–31). He suffocated from fumes during the eruption of Mount Vesuvius after sailing nearer to take a better look. Pliny the Younger (A.D. 62–113) was a Roman writer and orator. He was the nephew and adopted son of Pliny the Elder. He saw Mount Vesuvius erupt and wrote an eyewitness account of it (*Letters* 6, 16). The Anglo-Saxon epic poem *Beowulf* was written in England about A.D. 700, not long after the Sutton Hoo ship burial. It contains a description of the Danish king Scyld being laid to rest on a ship that is then pushed out to sea. Juan Rodríguez Freyle was a Spanish chronicler who wrote an account of the ceremony of the "Golden Man." This is probably the most reliable account, as Freyle learned about the ceremony from his friend Don Juan, a nephew of the last independent lord of Guatavita. Charles Brandon (1484–1545) was a soldier and brother-in-law of Henry VIII. Sebastian Manrique was a Catholic priest who observed the building of the Taj Mahal.

Page numbers in *italics* refer to captions and maps.

Alexander the Great 16, *16*
Alexandria lighthouse *14*
Alfred Jewel *5*
Alva, Walter 22, 24
Anastasius 33
Anglo-Saxon burial 33
Anthony Roll *40*
Artemisia 14
Aztecs 36

Barrow *13*, 47
Beowulf 33, 47
Brandon, Charles 40, 47
Brown, Basil 32
burial mounds 12, 32–33

Caravanserai 34
Carnarvon, Lord 6, 7
Carter, Howard 6, 7
chariots 12, *14*, 15, 28, 29, *29*
Chibcha 38, 39, *39*
Christian treasure 26, 27
Cleopatra 16, *17*
coffins *4*, *6*, 7, *7*, 23, *25*, 35, 47
coins 26, 33, *33*, 36, *36*, 37, *37*, 47
Colossus of Rhodes *14*
cremation 11, *16*, 17

Death mask 7
Derrynaflan treasure 26, 27
Dou Wan, princess 18–19, *18*, *19*
Drake, Sir Francis 36

Egyptian tombs 6–7, 46
El Dorado *4*, 38–39, *38*
Elizabeth I 36
Eskimo child *42*
Etruscan tombs *5*, 10–11, *10*, *11*

Freyle, Juan Rodríguez 39, 47
friezes 14, *15*

Gengis Khan 35
gilding *23*, *25*
gold jewelry 10, 11, *13*, *39*
Golden Man ceremony 38, *38*, *39*, 47
gun 40, *40*, *41*
Gur-i Amir tomb 34–35

Halicarnassus Mausoleum 14–15, *14*, *15*
Han Dynasty 18, 46
Hanging Gardens of Babylon 14, *14*
Helios statue *14*

Henry VIII 40, *40*, 46, 47
Herodotus 12, 13, 47
Howard, Sir Edward 40

Ice Man 42, 43, *43*
ice tombs 12, *12*, *13*, 42–43
Incas 36

Jade ornaments 18–19, *18*, *19*, 30, *30*, 31, 35
Jade Prince *5*, 18–19, *18*
jawab 45, *45*

Kaiserangst Hoard 26
keel 40, *41*

Lamp 19
lapis lazuli 7, 8
larnax 16, *17*
Lindow Man 42, *42*, 46
Li Si 28
Liu Sheng, prince 18–19, *18*, 46
Lords of Sipán 22-25, *24*, *25*

Madrassa 34
Manrique, Sebastian 45, 47
marble memorial 45, *45*
Mary Rose *5*, 40–41, *40*, *41*, 46
mausoleum *5*, 14–15, *14*, *15*, *34*, 44, *44*, 45, *45*, 47
Mausolus, king 14, *14*, 46, 47
Mayan god *30*
Mildenhall Treasure 26
Moche 22–25, *22*, *23*, *25*
Mongols 34, 35
mosque 45, *45*, 47
Mount Vesuvius 20, 46
Muisca 38
mummy *6*, 7
Mumtaz Mahal 44, *44*, 45, *45*
Mycenaean tombs *46*

Neanderthals 4

Ocho reales *36*, 37
Ötzi *5*, 42–43, *43*, 46

Pacal the Great *4*, 30–31, *30*, 46
peat bogs 26, 27, 42, *42*
Pérez de Quesada, Hernán 39
Philip II of Macedonia *5*, 16–17, *16*, 46
pieces of eight *36*, 37, 47
pirates 36, *36*, 37, 47
plaster cast *21*
Pliny the Elder 15, 47
Pliny the Younger 21, 47

Pompeii *5*, 20–21, *20*, *21*, 46
Posidonius 11, 47
privateers 36, 37
Pu-abi, queen 8–9, *9*
pyramids *6*, 14, *14*, 24, 46

Radiocarbon dating 42, 43, 47
Raedwald, king 33, 46
rhytons *26*, 27
Roman treasure 26, *26*
Royal Standard of Ur *8*
Rudenko, Sergei 12
Ruz, Alberto 30

Sacrifice 9, *22*, 23, 30, 31, *31*, 42
salvage operation 40, 41
sarcophagus *4*, 7, *7*, *17*, 47
Scythian tombs *5*, 12–13, *12*, *13*, 42
Sepúlveda, Don Antonio 39
Seven Wonders of the Ancient World 14, *14*
Shah Jahan 44, 45, *45*
Shih Huang Ti, emperor 28–29, *28*, 46
ships 32, *32*, 33, *33*, 36, *36*, 37, 40, *40*, 41, *41*
Sipán, Lords of *4*, 22–25, *24*, *25*
Spanish treasure *4*, 36–37, *36*, *37*, 46
surgeon's chest *40*
Sutton Hoo burial mounds *5*, 32–33, *32*, *33*, 46

Taj Mahal *5*, 44–45, *45*, 46, 47
Tamerlane, emperor *5*, 34–35, *34*, *35*, 46
tattoos 12, *12*, 43
Temple of Artemis *14*
Temple of Inscriptions 30–31, *31*
terracotta army *5*, 28–29, *29*
tholos *46*
Thracian treasure 27
Tibetan burial 4
Tomb of the Reliefs 10, *11*
treasure fleets 36–37, 46
Treasury of Atreus *46*
tumuli 10
Tutankhamen *5*, 6–7, *6*, *7*, 46

Ulugh-Beg 35
Ur cemetery *5*, 8–9, *8*, 46

Viking funerals 4

Wall hanging *13*
warrior-priests 22–24, *22*, *24*
Woolley, Sir Leonard 8

Zeus statue at Olympus *14*